The Yeats We Knew

Edited by FRANCIS MACMANUS

Memoirs by
PÁDRAIC COLUM
FRANCIS STUART
MONK GIBBON
EARNÁN DE BLAGHD
AUSTIN CLARKE

THE MERCIER PRESS
4 BRIDGE STREET, CORK

Published for Radio Éireann
by The Mercier Press
Summer 1965
Reprinted 1969

Printed in Great Britain
by C. Tinling and Co. Ltd.,
Prescot and London

THE YEATS WE KNEW

Contents

Introduction

Every autumn, winter and spring since September 1953, Radio Éireann has been broadcasting half-hour lectures, named in honour of Thomas Davis. Inspired by one of his famous sayings, 'Educate that you may be free', the aim of these lectures has been to provide in popular form what is best in Irish scholarship and the sciences.

Most of the lectures have been in series; many have been single broadcasts; some have been in English, some in Irish. In the comparatively short time that has passed since they were initiated, the lectures have dealt with many aspects and with many centuries of Irish social life, history, science and literature. The lecturers, distinguished for their special learning at home and abroad, have been drawn from many nations but mainly from Ireland.

The general title of some of the series provide an idea of the variety and scope of the lectures: Early Irish Society; Saint Patrick; Ireland and Renaissance Europe; Irish Battles; Science and the Nation's Resources; Irish Folklore; The Land and the People; The Shaping of Modern Ireland; The Celts; and The Integrity of Yeats.

Foreword

On 13th June, 1865, W.B. Yeats was born. The world came to know him as one of the greatest of poets; many of his contemporaries came to know him as a most impressive, enigmatic and infinitely interesting personality. In 1965, to mark the centenary of his birth, Radio Éireann broadcast a series of six memoirs in the form of Thomas Davis Lectures by men who were more or less closely associated with him. Some of these men admired him intensely. None was overwhelmed. At least two approached him with that native scepticism which is the salt of many Irish memoirs. The lectures appear in this book in the order in which they were broadcast, that is, with the exception of Frank O'Connor's which is not published as it was pre-empted for publication in the second volume of his autobiography. Readers will surely acknowledge a debt of gratitude to Pádraic Colum, Francis Stuart, Monk Gibbon, Earnán de Blaghd and Austin Clarke, for the portraits from memory of Yeats which they present. His deep variety is manifest in the variety of the portraits.

Francis MacManus

Pádraic Colum

My first meeting with William Butler Yeats was on the night of the last performance of A.E.'s *Deirdre* and Yeats's *Kathleen Ni Houlihan,* the plays that were the first offerings of the National Theatre Society which eventually became the Abbey Theatre. I was the youth who, in *Deirdre,* carried a spear and had a speech about Fergus whom Deirdre accused of 'Bartering his honour for a feast'. I was a player and so was Maud Gonne who played Kathleen ni Houlihan, and who was a party to Yeats's invitation to come to a hotel – his or hers – to discuss the draft of a play of mine. 'My first meeting' I say, but I had seen the poet at rehearsals and had more distant glimpses of him on platforms and on streets. A.E. and Yeats had furnished the initial plays of the theatre, but no other playwrights had shown themselves, and so Yeats was interested when Fay told him I was trying to write a play. I need not say how exciting it was for a beginner to have himself put in the rank of a possible dramatist for a National Theatre.

The Yeats whom I now met as a man of the theatre was getting on to his fortieth year. He had written *The Wind Amongst the Reeds,* and it was known that he was eager to pass from such tremulous kind of poetry to the more public kind that he would have to grapple with in the theatre. Therefore, it was at a developing period in his life that I was fortunate enough to meet the great poet. He was preparing himself for a new career – indeed I might say for a new sort of being. He was reading all the dramatists, including the dramatists of the day, Ibsen and Maeterlinck. I remember I spoke of these two dramatists with fervour. Yeats spoke a word of warning in that voice of his that had something oracular in it. 'We are obsessed with the translation...' He meant that the personal style that all great writers have was blurred in translation and that we mustn't give a complete adherence to the text. This is one of the illuminating things I remember from early conversations with one who said most revealing things about literature. That night, in a hotel whose name I have forgotten, I read to him and to Maud Gonne the little play I had shown our schoolmaster, Willie Fay. Yeats noted that there were too many people, too many motives in the opening. He made me aware that there was exposition in a play, and that the exposition had to be clear. He gave me a watchword – 'Clear the decks for action.' That was the first real directive I had been given for the writing of a play.

At this time, Yeats was still the youngish man of the velvet jacket and the flowing tie. To the Catholic intelligentsia who had, a few years before, picketted his play 'The Countess Cathleen', he was subversive. But that did not recommend him to the other side, the Ascendency side, the side of his father's friend, Professor Dowden. They had seen him from the site of the projected Wolfe Tone monument make a speech that was not at all in the spirit of Queen Victoria's Jubilee and denouncing that eminent lady in letters to the press. Percy French had Victoria, on her visit to

Ireland, retort in words that a head waiter committed to memory.

> There must be a slate, sez she,
> Off Willie Yeats, said she,
> Denouncing me crimes, sez she,
> In the *Irish Times,* sez she.

But the fact that two sides of the Irish public were hostile to him made this thirty-year old man interesting, and to be interesting, Yeats would probably have said, was the first duty of a public man. And Yeats wanted to be a public man. I fancy that if, at this stage, someone had said to him 'But you are a poet. Why want to be a public man?' Yeats would have told him that the entry into public life would give what he thought the entry into the theatre would give a poet, 'more manful energy'.

It was not his opinions alone that made him a marked man in the Dublin of the early 1900's. The tall, lank figure in black clothes, with the blue-black hair coming over his forehead, his frequent gestures and deliberate utterance, challenged and discomfited people. 'Pose' was a word that was often used about him. With reference to this word 'pose' I should like to say a word.

Yeats was a man who believed in style – or manner, if you like to call it that. 'Art is art because it is not Nature', said Goethe, and Yeats often repeated that saying. This insistence on art, style, manner, infuriated Dubliners, all except the sophisticated and certain members of the rising generation. People whose literary tradition went back to Thomas Moore and the poets of 'The Nation' felt affronted by his dismissal of 'The Minstrel Boy' kind of verse and by his downgrading Thomas Davis to the category of oratory rather than poetry. Speaking of verse in the Davis style, he said to me, 'I am leaving "The Spirit of the Nation" for my old age.' When I repeated this saying to an intelligent young man, he said furiously, 'The Spirit of the Nation will leave Yeats for its old age.' This aloofness of his may have been deliberate and due to the vocation that he felt in himself. But it may have been due to something in his character. His father once said to me, 'Willie is like his mother. She seldom if ever showed any sign of affection. I could be six months in Africa, and when I came back all she would say would be "Did you have your dinner?" ' 'But' the old reflective painter added, 'there's a Yeats side to Willie, too. He is expansive and he loves discourse.' At the time, he was comparing Willie the poet with his other son, Jack the painter – Willie's aloofness, Jack's liking for the commonality, Willie's discourse with Jack's laconic utterance. Yes, Willie was undemonstrative about everything except art and abstract ideas, and perhaps this contributed to the malice that was in Dubliners' talk about him. The elaborateness of his speech was also a theme for mockery. This elaborateness comes over in an interview reported by Gogarty between the young James Joyce and Yeats – an interview which may never have taken place. 'Joyce, the Japanese have a proverb: be brave in battle, be truthful to your friends, be courteous always. You are not courteous, Joyce. When Arthur Symons mentioned Balzac, you laughed.' But perhaps the way of accounting for the malice directed against a man whose gifts were known and whose purpose was enriching is the saying that is in the Bible – 'My heritage is to me as a speckled bird – all the birds of the air are against it.' Still, this discussion about the ways of one who was admitted to be a poet with the sacredness and mystery that has always surrounded the poet in Ireland, had another effect. His personality, his plans, his ideas were made current. And there was something about Yeats that rarely goes with the poet – the successful public-relations man, the one who made a theatre of amateurs playing in a hall that held only a hundred or so people into an institution, into what one never had before, an Irish theatre.

He was a great poet partly through his realisation that poetry should be personal but that it should also be related to some public effort. A poet whose life he admired, William Morris, had spoken sadly of the poet of his time as 'the idle singer of an empty day'. Yeats was determined to be not that sort of a singer. Poets are well served, he knew, when they have a cause, an ideal that brings them on the stage as spokesmen. He once said to me that the Catholic poets in England, Coventry Patmore and Francis Thompson, were fortunate in having a definite public. From his beginning he asked a public to recognise him as an Irish poet. –

> Know that I would accounted be
> True brother of that company
> Who sang to sweeten Ireland's wrong
> Ballad and story, rann and song.

But he also wanted to be a power in Irish public life. Remember that if the Irish coinage is stamped with creditable designs it is through Yeats the Senator working in committee. He was a capable man of affairs and was resolved to have his way in them. I remember that, during a dispute in the formative theatre group, a letter he wrote to A.E. which A.E. showed to me. Speaking of his own intention about the theatre, he left no doubt as to who was to be in control. 'The tools to him who can use them.'

He recognised in the theatre, whose nucleus was Fay's company, a real form of national expression. Quoting Victor Hugo, he used to say, 'In the theatre the mob becomes the people.' I am not here telling the story of the early days of the theatre, but my impressions of the Yeats who was taking over the theatre. He was able to fill with enthusiasm the members of this semi-amateur group. I remember the occasion of the re-organisation of that group. The great affirmation in that speech came through a poem he repeated – the poem of Lionel Johnson's that is dedicated to John O'Leary and begins, 'A terrible and splendid trust/ Heartens the host of Innisfail' and, as you will remember ends with.–

> A dream, a dream, an ancient dream –
> Yet ere peace comes to Innisfail,
> Some weapon on some field must gleam,
> Some burning glory fire the Gael.

He made our enterprise seem equal to Robert Emmet's and Wolfe Tone's when he repeated, the last, the significant verses.—

> That field may lie beneath the sun,
> Fair for the treading of an host,
> That field in realms of thought be won,
> Where armed minds do their uttermost.

> Some way, to faithful Innisfail
> Shall come the majesty and awe
> Of martial truth, that must prevail
> To lay on all the eternal law.

There and then he enlisted us for the field 'in realms of thought', for the martialness that was of the mind.

At the rehearsals of the Yeats play that we put on after *Kathleen ni Houlihan*, — it was *The King's Threshold*, rehearsals that were held at the back of a grocery shop in Camden Street, Yeats was often amongst us. He would read a poem that someone had sent him and speak to us about it. He was on the watch for the rise of a poet who would help to forward the enterprise – 'The Avatar', to use a word of his. And it was there that he brought us evidence of the Avatar's arrival, two short plays by a man none of us had heard of. The plays were 'The Shadow of the Glen' and 'Riders to the Sea' and the writer was J.M. Synge. One or two new players had joined what had been the Fays' company. They, like the older members, had taken lessons from Frank Fay or Willie Fay. I remember the rehearsal at which one of these neophytes came to the platform to say a few lines. Her movement, her gesture, her enunciation were assured and she had extraordinary distinction. Yeats turned to Willie Fay excitedly, 'Fay, you've got an actress.' She was Sara Allgood.

It requires practice to write verse which, spoken from the stage is intelligible to an audience. When Yeats wrote the opening speech for *The King's Threshold,* the King's speech of greeting to the poet's pupils, he did not yet know how to make a speech that has some complicated expression. The climax of that play has been changed since it was first put on, but that opening speech remains unchanged and is still impossible to make intelligible. It is a question of the timing of its delivery. Yeats was discomfited. I knew that the speech couldn't be made clearer no matter how the actor tried. I went to Yeats who was standing ruefully aside and said to him, 'The speech is frankly a public oration. What the audience will know is that the King is making a speech; it does not have to be intelligible line by line.' His head went up and his face cleared. Running across to Fay he said, 'Colum says that the speech is frankly an oration.' It was then given as an oration without any attempt to make it particularly intelligible. I like to think that the unaltered speech that we now read with all that talk about horses that draw the sun and the moon being welcome by someone for some fair woman's sake was due to my intervention.

Synge's plays were produced and also a play of mine which he thought was immature – as it was. But he had faith in me as a dramatist, and when I was finishing my next play, *The Land,* he had Lady Gregory invite me to Coole where we could discuss revisions

and developments in the play. By this time Yeats had
learned a good deal about the technique of playwrit-
ing, and I well remember one or two scenes in *The
Land* that profited by his professionalism. But I am
speaking of the poet and not of a play. In that beautiful house with its noble woods and lonely lake I saw
him without any of the pose that was mocked at in
Dublin. He was a good oarsman and we sometimes
rowed on the lake. The lake was in a picture he had
painted – a golden crown in deep water.–

> The golden crowns that kings had hurled
> Into deep pools when armies fled.

It was a picture that evoked something of the verse in
'The Wind amongst the Reeds' or 'Shadowy Waters'.
But that was a stage that he had passed through. He
told me that he was trying to get out of his poems 'the
reds and yellows that Shelley had brought back from
Italy'. Henceforth he was going to try to get into his
poems that grey of the West of Ireland – the stones
and clouds that belonged to Galway. How well he has
done that we know from the later poems of his.–

> The trees are in their autumn beauty,
> The woodland paths are dry,
> Under the October twilight the water
> Mirrors a clear sky.
> Between the brimming water and the stones
> Are nine and fifty swans.

I used to go through the woods with Robert Gregory

who shot pigeons there – we often had a grand pigeon-pie for dinner. Or I walked in the walled garden with Lady Gregory while she spoke to me of the guests of hers who had thrown wallflower seeds into the corners of the walls where there were now bunches of wallflowers. What a charming way of memoralising Douglas Hyde and Hugh Lane and many other illustrious visitors. And what can we say of the philistinism of an Irish government that let a house, beautiful in itself and so full of the history of our most creative generation, and woods that were so celebrated, be destroyed!

But William Butler Yeats is my subject. Naturally I was interested in the methods of work of a poet. In the morning he stayed in the large drawing-room, sitting before a table, or pacing about murmuring lines of verse that he had set down or was about to set down. Like many imaginative workers he had to tease himself into getting on with the job. At one time he used to smoke a cigarette between lines, but that gave him too much time off. Now he cut cigarettes into halves. The smoking of a half cigarette was the interval he now allowed himself. I told him that I thought of helping in some newspaper office for a while every day so as to give myself the discipline of a task that had to be done on time. There was no point, he told me, in doing this. The only discipline that mattered to the imaginative worker was the discipline he gave himself through his work.

In the drawing-room where we sat after dinner – Lady Gregory, W.B., Robert Gregory and myself, the conversation was natural and interesting. Yeats no longer made oracular pronouncements but spoke on all kinds of topics, gossiping with some humour on the coteries in London, repeating sayings of painters and writers. The son of a really great conversationalist, John Butler Yeats, he himself was a remarkable conversationalist. In the room across from us, the music room, Lady Gregory's nieces, sometimes played. I discovered that Yeats who was so varied in the music of his verse was absolutely tone deaf. I had heard him say that he liked a harp because it looked well-shaped. Now as we heard the music from outside the drawing-room, he said to me, 'What are they playing? Fiddle or piano?' I left Coole, bearing Lady Gregory's gifts – an enormous barm brack, and a large, well-cooked ham. Yeats was satisfied with what I had produced. Speaking to me as a counsellor, he said, 'Make yourself indispensable.'

There was more than one great moment in Yeats's life. To the honour of Ireland he was selected for the Nobel Prize. As he addressed an audience that included the King of Sweden and the members of the Swedish Academy he must have felt that this was a dazzling moment. And yet I think that the moment of achievement for him was the first night in which plays were performed in the Abbey Theatre. Irish dramatists and Irish players already had an international reputation. Now they were an institution. The audience for the plays that inaugurated the theatre were the elite of Dublin. Then there came on the stage that tall, darkgarbed figure whom they could now recognise for a standard-bearer. They knew he was a man who could make this an occasion they would remember. He raised his hand in the gesture so familiar to all who approached him. There was drama in the way he repeated lines from Spenser, lines over the gate of the Castle. 'Be bold; Be bolder still! Be yet more bold! But not too bold!' I will always remember that appearance and utterance of his as one of the great performances I had ever known.

And now for my last meeting with the poet who gave such greatness to his time. He was then living with his family in Rathfarnham, an ailing man. He consented to receive my wife and myself. We had been away from Ireland for some years. As compared with other times we had seen him, he was subdued. But in spite of the tiredness that he showed now and again he talked as a man with a continuing interest in what was creative in the world. He wanted to know more about certain contemporary poets whom he had seen or heard of, particularly of a German poet whom my wife had read, Stefan George. She was able to repeat some phrases from poems – he listened with much attention and made some comments. We left a stooped, white haired, courteous man, bringing with us a sense of grandeur. Here was one of the rare men in the world who had fully lived the creative, the intellectual life.

Pádraic Colum

Francis Stuart

During the years I knew Yeats I was so aware of him as the creator of poems that haunted me that I gave little thought to what kind of person he was, beyond a recognition of his generosity towards younger writers, which he showed by never failing to praise those of us with whom he felt some kinship, however slight. I was aware of a strange, contradictory person, whose every sentence and mannerism seemed controlled and formalised, a being not capable of spontaneity except perhaps when roused to defend a cherished principle, somebody whose studied humour I didn't find comic and for whom I had awe, admiration and a certain respect, but never, that I can recall, a sense of friendship or even the affection that a much older man can sometimes inspire in a young one. At the time this didn't strike me as particularly strange. I looked on Yeats as living in a world of his own, the dream world of his poetry, and being beyond ordinary human relationships. It was only long afterwards that I began to see him differently, and to suspect how unfulfilled and lonely he had been in the latter years.

My first contact with Yeats was a slight and indirect one but it has remained in my mind. I was a boy at Rugby School and our English master with whom we were reading 'The Countess Kathleen' wrote to him to elucidate some point in the play. A note came back from the poet in the spiky script I was to become so familiar with later, and was pinned on the notice board where I contemplated it with a kind of awe.

During the next few years my life was coloured by Yeats's poems. He himself seemed almost as remote and legendary as those other stirrers of my youthful imagination, Shelley, Wordsworth and Blake. So when, at eighteen, I married Maud Gonne's daughter, Iseult, and found myself in the circle of his friends it appeared to me as an extraordinary turn of events.

Before I actually met him, my wife told me stories about him, some from the time just before the 1914 war when he had stayed with her mother in their villa at Colville on the Normandy coast. It was there, she told me, that he had written her the poem 'To a Child Playing on the Shore'.

But the tone of most of her memories came as a shock to me. They seemed to show Yeats in a somewhat ridiculous light. It took me a time to realise that to a child, as Iseult had been at this period, Yeats would be a very queer phenomenon. Nobody had a less easy or spontaneous manner and to the not-always deep-seeing eye of a child he was bound to appear to give himself airs and certainly be a bore. So that Iseult had been pleased at his discomfitures such as when he had sat on a tarry breakwater in some new flannel trousers on which he'd set great store. And even more so when after listening to him relating one of his psychic experiences of the night before in which the scent of violets had been wafted across his bed, her mother interrupted to tell him she had broken a bottle of perfume in her room and for a time the whole house had smelt like a beauty parlour.

Even when Iseult told me how, a few years later, he had proposed to her, it was impossible for her to treat the episode seriously and she related it in a tone of banter. She never got over her early impressions. To her, and I think to Maud Gonne herself, Uncle Willie, as my wife called him, was an enigma with his deliberate ways, his carefulness about his clothes and about money on the one hand, and his passionate, romantic poems on the other.

My own first meetings with Yeats were after my release from internment during the Civil War in 1923. I had had a small book of poems, 'We Have Kept the Faith', privately printed and published, and I remember the shock it was to me when I realised that this strange and rather chilling figure with his eagle glance was talking about this little book. And not only talking about it, but telling us that the Royal Irish Academy had selected it to give a prize to. Of course I guessed that it was Yeats who had been the cause of this unexpected move on their part. I realised then, and later this was often borne out again, that behind the forbidding and pompous seeming air there was a great generosity of spirit.

He spoke to us (to Iseult rather than to me, sensing, I think, the depths of confusion he'd have put me in by addressing me directly) of one or two of the poems with that enthusiasm that could change his whole manner, giving it naturalness and warmth.

Later, at the ceremony at the Mansion House, I felt little of that touch of the ridiculous that Yeats's solemnity could so easily evoke, in having to go up to a dais and kneel while he placed a laurel crown on my head.

My mother-in-law had impressed on me not to refer to Yeats as Senator in my short speech of thanks, and this I refrained from doing, not out of nationalist reasons though, but because there seemed to me to be no greater honour than being plain W.B. Yeats.

Afterwards Yeats, Major Bryan Cooper (both in top hats and morning suits), G.K. Chesterton (why he was there I don't remember), Iseult and I, walked down Dawson Street to a restaurant called the Bonne Bouche for tea. Yet once at our table Yeats seems to have retreated (as he could when the atmosphere was unpropitious) into shadowy silence and all I recollect are a string of humourous anecdotes told by Chesterton and chuckled over by the almost equally enormous Major Cooper, while I, in loyalty to Yeats, tried to reflect his own absorbed and oblivious expression.

Being in his company (no matter how great an honour I may have felt it) was not a relaxation. In later years when he stayed with us at Laragh I avoided, if I could, being left alone with him. I could never be sure of finding the right responses to the kind of speculative talk he was given to. Sometimes, almost in desperation, I managed to say something that he would seem to find profound and enlarge on. But I always had the fear that I couldn't keep it up.

'Willie thinks you're a genious,' my wife told me, and this made me more than ever anxious to hit on the right conversational tone. For the truth was that I never found the company of Yeats anything but a strain as, I believe, did most if not all of his friends. There was little or no ease or lightness in the talk, his humour seemed studied and ponderous, the atmosphere had something formal about it. Not that I wasn't aware of being with somebody full of intellectual passion, whose great mental energy had no real outlet except in his work, and which, socially, scared off more people than it attracted. Of course there were always some literary snobs and sycophants who hung around him for the reflected prestige, but his real friends were few because few could breathe the strange, rarified atmosphere.

I recall remarking how scant the gatherings were at his Monday evenings (I think it was Mondays he and Georgie set aside to receive friends when they lived in Merrion Square). And Yeats himself complained of this lack of society in Dublin, though I imagine it was not much different when he lived in England.

Yeats himself wasn't unaware of the effect he often produced on his admirers. He told me of how Sean O'Casey had come to see him and had sat on and on after the six o'clock drinks and through the dinner to which he'd not been invited, too petrified to get up and go. He also knew the effect he produced – aloof, severe, romantic – on women. I remember how he pulled down the waistcoat of the beautiful fawn suit which is the one I always see him in, smoothing it over a belly that was becoming portly and remarking that the ladies set great store on his appearance. And this shrewd awareness of the reactions of those around him went with a genuine obliviousness and absent-mindedness in many other ways. So that when we stayed with the Yeats in the Merrion Square house, Georgie had to pin a notice on the door of our room to remind him that it was no longer his.

It was on one of our visits there that I told him about a periodical that Cecil Salkeld, Con Leventhal, Fred Higgins and myself were bringing out. I had got a rough lay-out of the paper from the printers and I showed him the rather amateurish-looking sheets.

The idea attracted Yeats and to our surprise and delight he offered to give us a new and unpublished poem of his to print in the first number. It was the poem 'Leda' and when I read it I realised that because of this poem our paper, which we called 'To-Morrow', would be of importance. But Yeats's interest in the project went even further. He wrote an editorial for us (not, of course, to appear above his signature though there was no mistaking the rounded, sonorous prose). In it he deplored the lack of any cultural standards in the new Irish State and in the Church in Ireland, and criticised the Bishops for what he called the 'rancid' style of their Pastorals. He went on to argue that had their faith been of anything but a timid and conventional sort it would have inspired their language and saved it from staleness and cliché. He contrasted them to Pope Alexander who had commissioned Michael Angelo to decorate the Sistine Chapel and thus manifested a vigour and wisdom now completely lacking.

I don't think we realised what a bombshell we were exploding when we printed this article, to say nothing of the poem with its strange, perverse eroticism. I know *I* didn't. 'To-Morrow', of which we had envisaged selling a very limited number in Leventhal's bookshop, was soon sold out. It was discussed and denounced, and was seen being read in such unlikely places as the dining-room of a hotel in Athlone and a country pub in Donegal. This delighted Yeats, who loved controversy and pitting himself against the less imaginative and daring. He was naturally opposed to what he saw as conformist and accepted attitudes, believing in what he called the 'aristocrat principle' by which he meant, I think, an original and speculative way of thinking as opposed to what was then the incoming tide of popular and democratic concepts. Or, as he put it:

> 'Not a fool can call me friend,
> And I shall dine at journey's end
> With Landor and with Donne.'

He saw in these writers the aesthetic and intellectual qualities he admired, and this caused him, I believe, to exaggerate their real merits. He sent us at about this time the complete works of Walter Savage Landor in something like a dozen volumes. Not having managed to work my way through even the first of them, I was a little apprehensive of our next meeting what I should say if Yeats launched out on one of his enthusiastic appraisals. But for some reason he hardly referred to Landor again, possibly because, having got all out of him that was grist to the mill, he dropped him, as was his way when something had served its purpose.

Yeats was not only opposed to a good deal in the new Irish State but he equally disliked the left-wing liberalism and rationalism that flourished in England between the wars. He told me that he had been asked to join in a petition signed by almost all the writers in

England protesting against the Reichstag Fire Trial then being conducted in Berlin, and said that he had refused. Not that, as I knew, he had any sympathy at all for totalitarianism but because he carried his love of individual freedom further than most of the signatories; to the point, in fact, where he became suspicious of the smugness and collective self-righteousness which they seemed to him to embody.

Out of the same instinct he talked with admiration of d'Annunzio who was much in the news at about that time, fascinated by a writer who was also a man indulging in dramatic and individual exploits. He quoted with approval d'Annunzio's dictum that it is necessary to live dangerously.

It was about this time too (in the middle thirties I think) that he came and stayed alone at the Royal Hotel, Glendalough, not far from where my wife and I were living. He wrote several poems there in the little back room built out over the stream from the lake, and sometimes read one to us when we visited him on an evening. His work was now becoming more erotic and concrete, just as his obsessions, as shown in his conversation, were more and more with phyical attributes: courage and sensuality. One of the poems was that about the bone that cried out on the shore.

He often surprised me by taking in small facts that I thought he would be bound to ignore. Unimportant coincidences would take his fancy in a way that I couldn't foresee. At dinner one evening we mentioned that the roast chicken was no doubt one of ours, as we had a contract to supply the hotel with poultry. And only a year or two ago, on looking through a volume of his letters, I came on one of them in which he had related this.

When we mentioned a writer we held in esteem he would hear what we had to say with that air of grave attention of his that made him a good if somewhat disturbing listener (making me always fear that what I had to say wouldn't come up to his obvious expectations). Then sometime later he would refer to the poet or novelist in question with a sentence usually beginning: 'My friends tell me...' and repeat the judgment of somebody whom I imagined as Edith Sitwell or another of the small circle of literary arbiters to whose taste he seemed, always to my surprise and irritation, to defer.

But I had an inkling that this was more of a defensive measure. Like many great artists Yeats was only really interested in, or absorbed by, what was of use to his own work, what could, in often strange and oblique ways, stimulate and inspire him. He had little interest in writers who, however good, were too far away from him to have this effect.

He garnered his harvest from many strange fields. From such unlikely experiences as playing the Senator and hobnobbing with Lord X and Z. And from public controversy he got a stimulation which intensified his life and indirectly his work.

I think the founding of the Irish Academy of Letters was something he undertook out of this instinct. As a weapon to wield against the Censorship laws it promised to involve him in the kind of passionate debates he thrived on. I still see him looming large and threatening on the small stage of the Peacock Theatre on the night of the Academy's inauguration, a glowering presence, one hand in the pocket of his fawn jacket, the other raised to stress what he was saying or to brush back the lock of dark-grey hair falling over the eagle brow, as he denounced what he looked on as the frightened and narrow attitude of the New State to literature. As one or two members of the audience got up and walked out (journalists from the more nationalist or pious section of the press) Yeats burnt with an even more intense indignation; and it was at such moments that, as a man, he was most admirable.

This was the nearest, perhaps, Yeats could come to the adventures of somebody like d'Annunzio, to that life of danger and violence that was the only kind (aestheticism having failed) that he could now reconcile with art. I sensed that Yeats wanted a life purged of its vulgar, trivial, coarse or even everyday qualities in order to bridge the gulf between it and his work. As he got older one could see this separation of art from life leading him into lonelier and lonelier paths. He tried to explain this by his phases of the moon and his theory of the antithetical self, but I couldn't help feeling, as he expounded it, that his semi-mystical philosophy had no real roots and was even sterile as a further impetus to his work. I think he was aware of this growing threat and in his conversation he lauded those qualities or vices which he lacked, using words like 'wild', 'violent', 'passionate', 'filthy', 'riotous', and so on. Just as in the conscious content of his work he tried to bridge the widening chasm by more and more 'realist' or 'brutal' images such as:

'Now that my ladder's gone,
I must lie down where all the ladders start
In the four rag-and-bone shop of the heart.'
But the impression one received was that, far from
his ladder having gone, he was constructing ever
longer and longer ones.

I think this sense of discord weighed on him and
drove him to try such solutions as his undergoing of
the rejuvenation operation, and his seeking out the
company of extroverts, who naturally, while being
flattered, found him more than they had bargained
for.

All my most vivid recollections of Yeats are either
the earliest ones of his visits to my mother-in-law's
house in St. Stephen's Green in the early 1920s, or during the period he lived in Merrion Square or from the
times he came to Laragh and Glendalough. Those be-
longing to the latter years, when he had a flat in Fitzwilliam Square and, even more, at the house in
Rathfarnham are fainter.

Whether this is because the inner fire was dying
down in him or because my own life and development
was taking me out of his strong and peculiar spell, I
don't know. The talk was as intense and intellectually
stimulating as ever.

Indeed I remember one evening in the Fitzwilliam
Square flat Georgie saying that if we kept him up talking beyond a certain hour he wouldn't sleep till morning. But for me a lot of the old, rare magic had gone
out of it and I was aware of somebody more and more
isolated and with less and less to fall back on except
the insubstantial consolation of world recognition.

37

He was more than ever concerned with the psychic. Like the magicians of old searching for the philosopher's stone, he seemed to be looking for concrete proofs of the supernatural. And apropos of the indication of such that he came across, he told a story of two interlocked rings made out of different kinds of wood that a woman friend of his had shown him. Then with the upward jerk of the head and the searching glance focussed so keenly on his listener, he announced like an ultimatum: 'That's your tangible, concrete miracle!'

Phrases of his, ennunciated in that sonorous chant, remain in my mind even when the argument and the context has faded. A typical sentence, for instance, beginning: 'The contemplative nun in her cell and the great lady in her boudoir...'

And side by side with what struck me as the growing desperation within, there were the indications of a physical crumbling. He lived in latter years in a hot-house degree of warmth. I recall him extricating his feet out of the enormous fur-lined slippers he wore in his study, coming with us to the door of his house at Rathfarnham and, although it was a warm summer day, shivering as he said good-bye.

He would sometimes talk with nostalgia to Iseult about the far-off days in France. He questioned her about her mother and at last came out with what I had a feeling had been on his mind. Would Iseult find out from her if she would care to see him again? I don't think they had met for many years. In fact there had been a certain rift and coolness between them, especially on Maud Gonne's side. She violently disapproved of his acceptance of the Free State status and his becoming a Senator. But even earlier I had heard her criticise him for what, now that he was married to a wealthy wife and had received the Nobel Prize, she looked on as his meanness. She had told me how, when she was in Holloway Prison in 1918, he had rented her Stephen's Green house and not only taken advantage of her circumstances to get it for a very low rent but allowed the pet rabbits he kept in the garden to eat all the plants!

However this might be, and Maud Gonne was a woman capable of much prejudice and unjust judgments, we knew the unlikelihood of her agreeing to see Yeats. But in the end Iseult managed to persuade her. They met at the Kildare Street club of which Yeats was a member, an arrangement that showed how completely out of touch Yeats was with his early love.

The reunion was not a success. My mother-in-law returned to Roebuck House in Clonskeagh with an ironic account of the meeting. By then Yeats appeared to her more ridiculous than ever. What Yeats thought of the haggard woman to whom remnants of great beauty still clung I don't know. She probably harassed him with the extreme politics that obsessed her as did his by now far-different preoccupations him. For she was not one to attune her talk to the company any more than could be. She told us they had tea in a gloomy room (in the hall, I think, because perhaps women were not admitted further) under a painting of some former viceroy, and that Yeats had had the insensitivity to introduce her to an Anglo-Irish peer of his acquaintance.

When, as I sometimes do, I look back and try to formulate an abiding impression of Yeats, I find I cannot do so by remembering him apart from his work. For what wasn't clear at the time was that the clue to much that was mystifying lies in the fact that his life and his poetry never merged. Or to put it another way, in spite of his interest in philosophy and mysticism (indeed I think this was an instinctive attempt to impose a meaning on his poems from outside) his work was not the expression of a deep, personal faith as it was say, for Rilke, Wordsworth or Blake.

In this, if in no other way, he was like Joyce. And in asking why it was that these two of our greatest artists were both, towards the end of their lives, deeply unhappy, it strikes me that it was just because of this; that in both their cases their work, so wonderful in texture, detail and artifice, lacks an inherent unifying vision of man.

Francis Stuart

Monk Gibbon

Towards the end of the Second World War Mr. T.S. Eliot flew to Dublin to deliver the first Yeats Memorial Lecture. I was standing in the crowded foyer of the Abbey Theatre about five or ten minutes before the lecture was due to begin when Sean O'Faolain, who was taking the chair, approached me. 'You must propose the vote of thanks.' I was in no mood to miss Eliot's interesting lecture while making notes for an oration of my own, but I retired to my seat in the brass-railed gallery, and in the four or five minutes which remained to me I jotted down certain lines of approach. From that dominating position in the gallery, immediately behind Yeats's widow, his daughter and his son, I was subsequently able to harangue, not only the whole audience, but Eliot himself on the stage; to chant some of the earlier poetry to them; and – in a sudden burst of confidence, influenced a little by the adjacency of those three relatives just in front of me – to tell the audience that I had seldom been in Yeats's presence for five minutes without irritating him to maddening point.

Perhaps the same confession is a necessary introduction now. The Yeats's band-wagon is overcrowded. Research students of every nationality spring up almost daily, thesis in hand. But those who knew Yeats personally are a diminishing body, and the longer one lives the greater one's rarity value therefore becomes, even though to some people I have seemed to be a traitor within the ranks. For that reason I am here.

But am I a traitor? Yeats's poetry, early, middle and late, must have given me as much pleasure as any man has ever received from it. He is the arch-magician in words of the era in which I have lived. The writers of real significance for us are those without whom we cannot even imagine life as we have known it. Cadences of theirs are woven into the very texture of our being. I find it impossible to envisage a world without *Innisfree*, without *Though you are in your shining days*, without *Outworn heart in a time outworn*, *Prayer for my daughter*, *What then, said Plato's ghost, What then?*; without *The Wild Wicked Old Man*. The man who wrote those poems was my relative. His sisters used to sign their letters to me 'your affectionate cousin Lily', 'your affectionate cousin Elizabeth'. There was a double relationship, a few generations back, a Terry one and a Butler one. As a young man my grandfather used to walk daily into Dublin with John Butler Yeats, the poet's father. They were both law students and once, when my grandfather had an exam, they departed from their usual route in order to avoid meeting a red-haired woman lest he should bring the candidate ill luck.

A little later when William Butler Yeats made his appearance on the scene in Sandymount my grandfather, who lived nearby, must have been amongst the first to offer his congratulations and to bend over the cradle. As a schoolboy, I knew my grandfather as an ardent lover of horses and a reader – if at all – of yellow backs, *The Strand Magazine,* Sexton Blake and Kipling. He died in 1909 almost certainly without having read even so much as a line of his distinguished relative.

I, however, was converted to Yeats's poetry at an early age by the gift of *Innisfree* as a wall-card from one of his sisters. Elizabeth had printed it but it was Lily who gave it to me and it was Lily who used to take me to the Abbey sometimes on Saturday afternoons, when I longed to see the poet himself but was always unlucky. When I did see him, I was aged twelve or thereabouts. It was one morning in a street in Dublin when shopping with my father, and the man in the broad-brimmed hat and with the black ribbon dangling from his pince-nez seemed to me both a little too fat and a little too deliberately absent-minded. 'That was your cousin, William Butler Yeats,' said my father, after we had safely passed him. I was a little disappointed. I had no objection to a man looking the part of the poet but I had an uneasy feeling that Yeats felt that it was *his business* to look the part. That was a different matter altogether.

Yeats's relationship with his two sisters was a curious one. 'I have two sisters,' he told Sturge Moore. 'One is an angel, the other a demon.' Both played a very appreciable part in smoothing his path as a writer. But the one who did most in that respect was the one whom he found it hardest to get on with, not because she had a mind of her own – for every member of that remarkable family had a mind of his or her own – but possibly because anyone who co-operated with W.B. was expected to do so on his terms; he found it hard to brook opposition. Elizabeth Yeats ran the Cuala Press. It was the successor to the

Dun Emer Press whose founder and owner, Miss Gleeson, Yeats had presumably found insufficiently tractable. Both hand-presses had come into existence to publish early limited editions of Yeats's own work and the work of a few of his friends. Elizabeth Yeats – or Lollie as she preferred to be called – has left her own memorial in these hand-printed volumes. She had no say in what was printed, and there were frictions, which may have grown more frequent as time went on, although actually both sisters were tied by bonds of the most undeviating loyalty to their famous relation. Yeats might say to his wife in later days, 'I'm meeting Lollie at the Shelbourne this morning. We're going there, because then we won't be able to shout at each other.' But no amount of shouting could lessen Elizabeth's pride in her brother. The whole family had learnt at a very early stage – almost certainly from John Butler Yeats himself – to regard Willie as a genius, and their respect for him never faltered.

I said once to Jack Yeats, as we sat together in his studio, something about the arrogance which W.B. could display on occasions. And in his entirely gentle and oblique way Jack came immediately to his brother's defence, hinting that it was a result of the humiliations which the poet had had to share in his youth, when family cash was always short and fame still very far off. But the picture which Katherine Tynan draws is of a young man quite indifferent to material considerations. I think it would be true to say that the poet came into the world with a good deal of latent pugnacity in his composition. Lily Yeats told me how a governess of theirs used to say, 'Everything is all right in the nursery until Willie comes home and then the fighting begins immediately.' Yeats was a fighter. I can imagine him enjoying his participation in *The Playboy*. It was probably a sharp-relished moment in his life, rather than an infliction.

I had seen the poet once, but it was ten years or more before I was to see him again. Home on leave from serving with the 31st Division in France in 1917, I bought the eight vellum-backed volumes of Bullen's Stratford Head Press edition of his works out of my pay as a subaltern, and directed my father to leave the first volume with Lily Yeats who was to get her brother to sign it for me. She did so. In microscopic handwriting on the first page are to be read now his signature and the two lines

> I have heard the pigeons in the Seven Woods
> Make their faint thunder

an allusion possibly to the considerably greater din which I was then hearing from the 16 inch guns in front of Arras. Yeats was not the perfect quarry when it came to autographs. Years later I asked both him and A.E. to sign copies of photographs which the Irish Times had taken of them. Russell signed in friendly fashion on the mount immediately below the photograph; but W.B. wrote his name on the very darkest part of the print itself where there was no danger of anyone save its owner ever suspecting the existence of a signature.

After the war Yeats came for a time to live on Sydenham Road in my father's parish of Dundrum.

One of Yeats's children – I think I am right in saying – was baptised by my father. The poet had only two topographical influences in his life, Sligo and Dublin. They were a part of his being, Sligo in childhood, Dublin as an art student with A.E. and afterwards in the early days of the Abbey and in old age. Nothing of London, where he lived for a number of years, nothing of Oxford, nothing certainly of Dundrum passed into him and became a part of him, as places become a part of ordinary individuals. To a greater degree than any other man in my experience, Yeats *created* his own environment, rather than took on colour from one already in existence. Even in the case of Coole Park I suspect that it became Yeatsland when he was there – a metamorphosis which no doubt had the full approval of Lady Gregory. And his stay in Dundrum though it brought him within a mile or so of his sisters, and, probably, while it lasted kept the poor Cuala Press in a state of very considerable tension, was, like so much else, a biographical irrelevance as far as the poet was concerned.

I was teaching in Switzerland at this time but even had I been at home it is most unlikely that I would have made the poet's acquaintance. That did not happen until he was living in Merrion Square. Plunkett and others had founded the *Irish Statesman* and put A.E. in charge of it and a poem of mine published therein had met with Yeats's approval. 'Who is Monk Gibbon?' he had cried down the stairs to Lily one morning; and she had replied, 'He is your cousin, Willie Gibbon,' not a very satisfactory classification, seeing that family ramifications were something quite outside his cognizance. His approval of my poem however was passed on to me, via Lily and my father, and I was told to call upon him when I next returned to Ireland.

The Yeats whom I met then and whom I knew thereafter for a certain number of years was the penultimate Yeats, the Yeats of the mid-twenties, the senatorial Yeats, re-patriated, re-established in concord with A.E., happy in his role of a public figure, and leagues removed from the gawky art-student of his earlier Dublin period. I doubt if his friends in youth, if they had been able to peer forward into the future, could have recognised him as he was now. I knew from Katherine Tynan that he had undergone a sea-change, and one not altogether approved by her. His fashionable and titled London acquaintances, she implied, had meant that the gentle, shy and altogether humble neophyte of literature that she had once known had vanished altogether and left not a wrack behind. Certainly humility is hardly the word that one would associate with the later Yeats.

We are up against one of the more interesting problems of personality, and in an acute form. Philip Toynbee, commenting recently upon Sartre's excursion into autobiography and on the French writer's savage rejection of himself as child and as small boy, has said, 'Self-hatred is at least as damaging an emotion as self-love, and we owe, I think, a very definite loyalty to those fragmentary and remote beings who are at least the progenitors of our present selves. We owe them the loyalty of admitting that they were, in however strange a sense, ourselves; that what we ex-

perienced of them was from inside and not from outside; and that there is in a human life, an unspeakable
continuity of identity.' Sartre has not conceded this
loyalty, and I don't think that Yeats ever conceded it
either. I think he had broken off the relationship with
his past self. A.E. was the only person who ever gave
me the impression that he was conscious of a continuity of identity in Yeats. To him the poet was still
'Willie Yeats', the boy who long ago shared his belief
in fairies and who – so Miss Yeats once told me – had
discussed with him over the ashes in their basement
kitchen range the arcane forces which could perhaps
explain a mushroom's rapid growth. Indeed one of the
reasons why A.E. slightly irritated Yeats – and I think
he did often slightly irritate him – may have been because he insisted on clinging to this earlier individual;
whereas the poet himself wanted to discard him and to
thrust him back into the past. This diversity of approach to his adolescence had various ramifications.
I always suspected Yeats of being subconsciously
jealous of A.E. It seemed to me that they had both set
out together upon the road of mystical enlightenment,
but that Yeats had very soon turned aside into the
by-ways of magic and symbolism. Whereas A.E.,
shedding the extravagances of some of his earlier convictions and fortified by a stronger moral purpose,
had continued steadfastly on the path of enlightenment and had become the sage. I can claim Mrs.
Yeats's support here in her remark to her husband
after A.E.'s death 'A.E. was the nearest you or I will
ever know to a saint. You are a better poet than he
was; but you are not a saint.' Indeed W.B. seemed to

endorse that verdict himself by quoting it in a letter to a friend.

But the cleavage in Yeats – which of course extended to his poetry and is regarded by so many critics as a sort of watershed separating the great later poetry from what they consider the relatively negligible, earlier work – may have had other causes besides this abandonment of the mystical quest on which he had once briefly embarked with his friend, Sex, and his attitude to women had something to say to it. Another reason is suggested for it in a very revealing remark which he once made to L.A.G. Strong. He said, 'In my youth I was shy and awkward and terrified of any gathering. Then I read in that book which I still think the wisest of all books, Wilhelm Meister of Goethe, the following words: "The poor are. The rich are but are also permitted to seem". Thereupon I set myself to acquire this necessary technique of seeming. I attended athomes and soirees and dinner parties and gatherings of every kind until I had lost my awkwardness, and had acquired the technique of seeming.'

This seems to me an astonishing confession for a great man to make. The technique of seeming. It is difficult for those who are untroubled by shyness to realise what an affliction it can be. I have noticed in a number of shy people a sort of angry resentment against anyone who came into the world with more assurance than they themselves possess. But to cure one's shyness by creating a deliberate façade, that seems to be tampering with the integrity of personality which one expects in the great artist.

Until I read this testimony of Strong, fairly recently, I had always imagined that Yeats's air of aloofness was a self-protective measure adopted mainly to defend the poetic consciousness and to keep the intrusive world at a safe distance. And, though I disliked it, it seemed justifiable and praiseworthy. It was a continual affirmation of the right of a poet to be solely himself. But now it appears that this was a measure to enable him to meet the world, rather than to escape from it, and this – if it was the case – would explain why one could not help being slightly irritated by what always savoured of pose, even though one might condone it as poetic pose. Strong tells us that he was an extremely shy man. If it is correct, one can only say that Yeats concealed it well from strangers behind a mask of slightly arrogant superiority. Even his geniality was a little too olympian.

To say this shows that I never penetrated – as others claim to have done – behind the poetic mask to the human individual. Again it is Leonard Strong who suggests a possible explanation. He says, 'Yeats could not abide reverence. It made him tongue-tied, it forced him at once into his official manner. Towards the end of his life his best friends were young men who treated him as an equal and told him unseemly stories. He had a relish for the unseemly and some of his own stories were Rabelaisian!' Could not abide reverence? If that was the case then I must have exercised the worst possible influence upon him, for I was an idolator of his poetry. And to me, even in his own home and amongst intimates like A.E., Lennox Robinson, Walter Starkie and Gogarty, Yeats always seemed tied to an official manner, instigated quite possibly by my own initial reverence and by the very fact that where both he and A.E. were concerned, I was unavowedly in search of a messiah. This didn't trouble A.E. in the least, because to some degree he was a messiah, a very human messiah, who would let drop a phrase of Patanjali and send you home fortified in spirit; but it was clearly not the way to win favour with W.B.

Though I did not immediately realise it and though I had started with a favouring wind behind me – a poem approved – an invitation to dinner – and an open invitation to his Monday evenings in Merrion Square the auspices were really all against me; I was reverent, which was unforgiveable, I was talkative which is always a grave disadvantage, and, in my search for truth and hunger for discussion – a hunger probably accentuated by residence abroad – I did not hesitate to cross-examine Yeats from time to time upon the logical sequence of his ideas. He was a bad subject for such cross-examination. He much preferred to throw out the striking phrase and leave it at that. The phrase could take care of itself. He was a poet and not a logician.

Nevertheless for a time I enjoyed his favour. I could go to his Monday salon whenever I wished. Salon is perhaps the wrong word for a gathering of four or five old friends together with an occasional young man, like Lyle Donaghy or myself. A.E. was my hero and he was nearly always there on these occasions which was perhaps a disadvantage. Strong has said, 'Of all men and women I have met, A.E. met life with the greatest serenity.' It was difficult not to contrast A.E. the sage, with W.B., the newly-made senator and slightly unconvincing man of the world.

I realised my privilege, but I suppose I was opinionated then, as I am opinionated now; and to be opinionated in youth is not always the best way to win favour with the elderly. Nevertheless Yeats could be kindly. He advised me strongly not to go and sit at the feet of Gourdjieff, in his institute at Fontainbleau, where Katherine Mansfield had died. 'Take the advice of an old man. I've seen a lot of that kind of thing –' and he went on to say that it tended to end in a sort of priestcraft. This was a big admission from the one-time Rosicrucian. I took his advice, paying only a brief afternoon visit to Fontainbleau, where in any case Gourdjieff was incapacitated with a broken leg and busy writing a book which, one of his disciples told me, he proposed to call 'Beelzebub's talks to his Grandchildren'.

The poet could give me his friendly advice, he could invite me to his house, he could write me kindly and thoughtful letters about two of my books which I had sent him but he could never overcome my awe of him or a certain prim tendency to compare him to his disfavour with A.E., and to disapprove his slightly bawdy man-of-the-world pose which came out most strongly when he was in Gogarty's company. Nor could he silence me or satisfy my ravenous hunger – the hunger of youth – for a doctrine, a theory, a creed which might throw a little light upon the mystery of existence. When one asked A.E. for bread he gave you bread, the bread of the Bhagavadgita or of Patanjali or of some nameless sage, like the one who had said – 'All lost oil burns in the lamp of the King' – a wonderful all-embracing phrase in which to gather up life's failures and misfits and all the apparent wastage of human personality which would nevertheless one day be justified in the divine scheme. But when one asked Yeats for bread, he did not actually give you a stone, but he gave you a beautifully polished pebble of phraseology, striking in its originality, but not exactly the sustenance which the soul sought at that moment. Of course he could say most brilliant and courageous things. I was not there when he remarked to two English dons, 'I can't see what you think you are achieving. You seem to be busy with the propagation of second and third and fourth hand opinions upon literature. Culture does not consist in acquiring opinions but in getting rid of them.' If I had been there I hope I should have applauded. I would certainly have appreciated that other brilliant remark, to an Oxford undergraduate who had told Yeats that he was contemplating a change of faith, 'In religion never leave your father's house until you have been kicked down the stairs.'

I have told in my book *The Masterpiece and the Man or Yeats as I knew him,* how our relationship went from bad to worse until I had become – as he said – 'one of the three people in Dublin whom I dislike – Dunsany, because he's rude to his wife in front of the servants, Monk Gibbon because he is argumentative and Sarah Purser because she's a petulant old woman.' Yeats had other personal reasons for disliking Dunsany and Sarah. They had stood up to him on occasion. But in my case it was a true bill. Lollie probably only made things worse by defending me to him and by begging me not to argue when I next saw him. 'W.B. doesn't like being argued with,' A.E. could say to me. 'You are the only person in Dublin who argues with Yeats. He ought to be grateful to you.' Did I ever argue with him I ask myself now, or did I just ask embarrassing leading questions in the manner of Rosa Dartle? I fell further and further from grace. If I kept silence in his company I was a bore. If I spoke I was maddening. Finally I toppled utterly from grace by publishing a book on the wrapper of which Jonathan Cape had printed a highly appreciative letter to me from A.E. This volume, unlike the others, was not acknowledged.

The effect of *The Masterpiece and the Man* upon Frank O'Connor was to make him feel that I was the typical individual with a grievance. But O'Connor is not quite fair to me. He has left out my one big grievance – the attempt to take from me what A.E. had himself entrusted to me, the posthumous editing of his journalism. Moreover O'Connor himself, in a lecture to the Yeats Summer School has admitted that Yeats could be, and often was, a bully. Even Strong, his ardent admirer says, 'In contention Yeats was unscrupulous and adroit.' I was to receive in full measure a striking illustration of both these qualities. I would have been less than human if I had not resented it.

There are very few disagreements in life which can be said to be inevitable, but I am not sure that mine with Yeats was not one. I placed him upon a pedestal as a poet, but he abhorred all such reverence. I subconsciously reproached him for not being a saint; but after all a man is free to choose his vocation. I challenged his philosophic statements with the earnestness of youth; and, if he could read my thoughts which I always very much hoped he could not, he must have realised that I was continually making comparisons to his disadvantage with the serene A.E. As Lily Yeats once said to me, 'You are afraid of him.' Yes, exactly, afraid of him; but by no means sufficiently afraid of him to keep my mouth shut when I considered one of his pronouncements illogical. When it came to opposition Yeats was at his worst. He lacked fundamental magnanimity and he was as ruthless as those who are sensitive themselves can often be. He has unveiled his mind, but not his personality to us in his writings. Did anyone know him really well, except possibly the members of his own household? I doubt if A.E. did. Perhaps Gogarty did. Perhaps Strong did. But he has left us a tireless memorial of himself in his poetry, and, before that, I uncover.

Monk Gibbon

Earnán de Blaghd

Although I often met Yeats, particularly at the Board-Room table in the Abbey Theatre, and although I took part in many discussions with him, I feel that perhaps I can offer only a worm's eye view of the man. Everyone who can read, may, according to his capacity, form an opinion of Yeats's work. But I do not know whether there were very many who knew him really well personally. He always seemed to me to be an aloof man, who, even when he was being genial and sociable, never fully unbent. His air of being withdrawn may have indicated no more than the abstraction of a dedicated writer, and, in certain kinds of select company, he may have inspired much affection as well as that admiration which, in not a few cases, verged upon awe. But I was often struck by the way in which people, who were obviously impressed by his genius, failed to show kindly personal feeling for him. When at Yeats's repeated invitation, I hesitantly joined the Abbey Board, knowing that as a consequence of becoming a member of it, I must relinquish the tenuous connection which I still had with active politics, I was visited at my home by the other new Directors, Fred Higgins and Brinsley Mac-Namara. They wanted to arrange that the three of us should act together on the Board. When I not only declined to be a member of any 'cave' but added that I regarded Yeats as the inspirer and real founder of the Abbey and that, however I might argue as a member of the Board, I should never go the length of voting against him, they both proceeded to tell me that I was altogether too simple-minded to deal with a man like Yeats. They said that I obviously had no idea of his craftiness, of the complexity of his mind, or of his capacity for using people for his own ends. I was taken aback by the vehemence of their talk. But I did not think that, in the case of the men mentioned, anything like subconscious jealousy was at the bottom of their iconoclastic attitude towards my image of Yeats.

I remember, however, talking to another literary man who astonished me by seeming almost to hate Yeats, whom he compared to a great towering widespreading tree, which was stunting and obscuring everything around it by keeping the sunshine from it, and depriving it of attention. In his case, I judged that a somewhat lunatic jealousy was at work. My two new colleagues on the Abbey Board who wanted to create an organised opposition to Yeats's views and policy may not only have been free, as I believe, of jealousy, but must also have been free of any idea that he underestimated or impeded their work. I did not return to the subject later to inquire why they, who knew Yeats so much longer and better than I did and who acknowledged his greatness, appeared to have no feelings of cordial goodwill towards him, especially as he had shown confidence in them by putting them on the Board. Later on, however, it occurred to me that their attitude may have come as a reaction against a concentration, on his part, on his art and ideals which excluded true and close friendship from his relationship with most of those who were in his circle.

Dr. Richard Hayes, who had been for a long time on the Board of the Abbey Theatre before I joined it, had a great but somewhat cynical admiration for Yeats's conduct in the chair. He told me that when he saw Yeats guiding and controlling the Board, he was reminded of a wily old Chairman of a Board of Guardians smoothing over differences, preventing splits and leading his fellow members to the conclusions which he thought best. I soon saw the resemblance which struck Dr. Hayes; but it was superficial. I think Yeats dominated the Board because he had clear well-considered views on practically every issue that could arise, because he argued every point equably and reasonably and because his prestige and air of lofty detachment gave his views added authority. He never allowed anything to deter him from doing what he thought necessary for the good of the Theatre, or, to rush him into precipitate action. The big split between Sean O'Casey and the Abbey Board, which followed the rejection of *The Silver Tassie,* was still unhealed when Yeats heard that O'Casey was ill in hospital. He went to see him as if no hard words had ever passed between them. He came away having promised that the Abbey would now perform *The Silver Tassie* and having got permission to do it as well as *Within the* Gates.

Again, when Yeats made up his mind that Lennox Robinson's lengthy period of distinguished service as producer in the Abbey should end, and a new man be appointed, he did not allow years of friendship and comradely co-operation to deflect him from his purpose. He first enlarged the Board, taking advantage of a seasonal increase in the ordinary public criticism of the Abbey to secure acceptance of his nominees, and agreeing that the new Directors should be without shares, and therefore easy to let go at a General Meeting of the Company. Once the new Directors, who had all been calling for changes in Abbey policy, were in office, Yeats proposed that a new producer with different experience and a fresh outlook should be appointed for a period. Through the good offices of John Masefield, Yeats found Hugh Hunt, a very young man who had produced for the Oxford University Dramatic Society, and invited him over. Naturally Lennox Robinson was deeply hurt by being ousted, on the advice of a colleague with whom he had for many years been on the best of terms.

I felt that only a highly conscientious and devoted man and only a man with a good deal of iron in him could have taken action so hard on a colleague with whom he had no quarrel. Lennox Robinson was a master-producer in some respects. No one could be better than he was in the elucidation of character or in helping players, to convey temperament and obsessions or to indicate hidden or subconscious motives. But the establishment of the Gate Theatre and the work of Hilton Edwards and Micheál MacLiammóir caused Dublin theatregoers to want productions in which there was more stress on grouping and lighting and dressing than had been usual in the Abbey. Hugh Hunt coming fresh to the Company without preferences or prejudices got some of the results that are possible for the new broom. He insisted on the installation of additional lighting facilities and that the

Abbey which had not previously had a full-time designer and scene painter should appoint one. Yeats, of course, gave Mr. Hunt any backing he needed.

A year or so later, Brinsley MacNamara, who had a strange irrational dislike of O'Casey's plays, did a thing which aroused Yeats's fiercest indignation. Encouraged, or led to forget himself, by some outside criticism of *The Silver Tassie* which the Abbey had just put on, Brinsley delivered himself of a diatribe against the play. And of course, the newspapers made the most of the intriguing situation thus created. Yeats summoned a special meeting of the Abbey Board which, unfortunately, I was unable to attend at short notice. Dr. Hayes, who told me about it afterwards, relished the proceedings immensely. Yeats was at the top of his form telling Brinsley that he had disgraced himself and thundering a demand for his instant resignation from the Board. At the regular meeting of the Directors held a day or two afterwards, Yeats was his usual calm self, but was determined that Brinsley must go. He proposed that special meetings of shareholders be summoned to dismiss him. When I suggested, as an immediate measure, that for the next six months the Board should delegate all its powers to a sub-committee consisting of six of its seven members, thus depriving Brinsley at once of all opportunity to participate in the work of the Theatre, Yeats accepted the idea. Brinsley sent in his resignation next day. Yeats, in spite of his indignation against MacNamara, was so pleased to be relieved from the necessity for expelling him, that he designated me to preside at meetings of the Board thereafter if he should be absent.

I do not remember any great differences of opinion about plays during the years in which I sat with Yeats on the Abbey Board. He frequently talked about the very bad plays which had been produced in the Abbey in its early years. They were put on, he said, because nothing better was available at the time. Before I became a Director of the Abbey, I had found myself getting tired of George Shiels's somewhat acid comedies, not realising that, for years, they had been an important factor in saving the Abbey from bankruptcy. I suggested that the Theatre should perform them much less frequently. Yeats promptly disagreed. He insisted that Shiels's plays were good: 'Rough work but good,' he said.

He was determined that no play should ever be produced in the Abbey which was likely to hurt the sincere religious feelings of anyone. Great as was his admiration for Synge, he had never permitted *The Tinker's Wedding* to be played in the Abbey because the representation of the priest in it would offend Catholics in the audiences. Soon after I became a director, new Irish plays worth production were very scarce, and it was proposed to go outside for something to fill the gap. A play giving an unflattering picture of Mary Baker Eddy, Founder of the Christian Science movement, was recommended. It seemed suitable as a stop-gap and likely to bring in some revenue. Directors generally were willing to have it done, but Yeats voted against its production. He was not going to have a play performed in the Abbey which would offend the susceptibilities of Christian Scientists, however few of them might see it. The matter was discussed at some length by the Board and Yeats made it plain that in the earliest days of the Abbey he had decided on his attitude and resolved that no matter what his religion, no one, Catholic, Protestant, Jew or Mahommedan should ever have to sit in the Abbey and hear things which he held sacred being derided or insulted.

Yeats was always against plays embodying crude propaganda. Once, during his absence from the country, a play was rejected by the Board, partly on the ground that it contained too much anti-clerical propaganda. And an attempt was made on his return to Ireland to induce him to ask the Board to reconsider its decision – the play was *The White Steed* by Paul Vincent Carroll. Yeats not only refused to disagree with the majority of the Board but gave a dissertation on how easily a literary work might be spoiled by the creeping effects of propaganda. I do not imagine that in this case Yeats was acting the part of the good senior colleague and throwing the protection of his mantle over the juniors on whom he had placed responsibility for carrying on in his absence. A matter of high importance was involved. A play by a major dramatist had been rejected. If Yeats had considered the Board mistaken he would not have hesitated to take steps to have the error rectified. However, when minor decisions were in question, it did appear to me that Yeats behaved, on occasion, as a good team-worker willing to support the action of the majority, by refusing to re-open a decided case.

In regard to plays generally, especially the work of

new writers, his attitude was benign. Perhaps many years of often-disappointing search for a sufficiency of good work by Irish writers and of deferred hope for the appearance of another dramatic genius, had made him more eager than he had been in earlier years, to see signs of originality, of developing power or of instinct for the theatre in writers who, on the surface, did not appear so very promising. Consequently, there was not at Board meetings any appreciable difference of view-point between Yeats and other members of the Board, on the plays which came before us. Perhaps the only exception concerned the plays of his brother, Jack Yeats. These quaint rambling compositions had a strange charm and indeed reminded one of certain pictures which delight the eye and intrigue the mind, though it is with difficulty and some uncertainty that recognisable figures or objects can be discerned in them.

A couple of Jack Yeats's plays were performed, years later in the Peacock Theatre or for a night or two in the main auditorium of the Abbey. They were warmly received by somewhat atypical audiences, members of which saw or professed to see things in them that were hidden from ordinary theatregoers. When it was found that one of them was too long and would have to be cut, to let the final curtain come down before too many people had rushed from the auditorium to catch the last buses, an actor averred that cutting would be quite easy. All that was called for, he declared, was to determine roughly what number of words had to come out to bring the play down to a convenient length and then to calculate how many pages they would fill. Thereupon ten, twenty, or fifty pages, as might be appropriate, could be taken at random and simply torn out, without audiences either noticing the joins or being conscious of gaps in the narrative. Most Directors felt that Jack Yeats's plays had some sort of quality and were not indisposed to try one of them on the public, partly as a gimmick and partly in the hope that Jack Yeats's name and his fame as a painter might draw substantial audiences to the theatre for a week or so. When the proposal was made at a Board meeting, however, W.B. Yeats pronounced firmly and curtly against it. And nothing more was heard during W.B. Yeats's life-time about the production of either *In Sand* or *La-La-noo*.

I never heard Yeats talk about spiritualism or any form of mystical belief or give any indication of interest in phenomena of a supernatural kind such as, we are informed, fascinated him. As a member of the Abbey Board, he was always the cautious, cool-headed business man, the sober confident literary connoiseur with a tolerant appreciative outlook and occasional enthusiasms but with a magisterial distaste for the shoddy and vulgar.

National or political issues did not arise in discussions at Board meetings. Without anything being said, however, the atmosphere left no doubt that everything done was being offered for the honour and renown of Ireland. In all my encounters with Yeats it seemed to me that there was conscious patriotism behind his actions and attitudes. I think, however, we need not consider him very seriously as a practical politician. He was not capable, in public affairs, of offering that firm resistance to a romantic personality or a romantic plan which is often the test of the politician who deserves to survive or to preserve his influence.

Though he professed to dislike personal involvement in controversy Yeats had no hesitation about coming out in opposition to the popular view or what he conceived to be the attitude of the mob. His stand for the freedom of the theatre from mob censorship was whole-hearted and uncompromising. I was in the Abbey on the night of the first performance of *The Playboy*. It was the first occasion on which I saw a queue outside the pit door awaiting its opening and it was the last time such a queue was seen for several years. Whatever kudos the *Playboy* row may have gained for the Abbey abroad, its effect at home was to drive away a great part of the following which had been gradually built up. That, however, was a small loss compared with what would have been suffered if a puritanical mob censorship had been made effective. Although Yeats had been associated, to some extent, with advanced nationalism and had been a friend and admirer of John O'Leary the Fenian leader, he did not hesitate to bring the police into the Theatre and to point out to them the disturbers whom they should arrest. After a week of arrests and fines the *Playboy* row was over, and there was no further attempt at communal censorship for a long time. On one occasion Yeats by a timely intervention averted a threatened disturbance. Norreys Connell's one act play *The Piper* got its first performance on Thursday 13th February 1908 when W. F. Casey's three act piece *The Man Who Missed the Tide* was produced for the first time. There was no hostile reaction to *The Piper* that night, but on Friday night it evoked a good deal of hissing as *The Playboy* had done on its first night a year previously. For the third performance of *The Piper* on Saturday afternoon, the auditorium was crowded, some people having come to see the play and others having come, as they would have said, to enjoy the fun. I was one of those who went both to see the play and to observe the disturbance which I believed would develop. Before the curtain went up, however, Yeats came out in front of it and made a very adroit speech. He would not attempt, he declared, to say what the author meant. The play was the author's own statement of that. But he would venture to tell us what he saw in the play. He saw the eternal heroic aspirations of the Irish people embodied in the character of The Piper. Then he came down to Black Mike whose cry 'God damn Father Hannigan' could well have been the spark which would start a blaze of anger in the auditorium. Yeats told us that he saw in Black Mike the embodiment of the men of burning sincerity, of the men who took action to achieve Irish freedom while others indulged in unending fruitless talk. In Black Mike he saw Robert Emmett and Parnell and all who had been willing to sacrifice themselves for Ireland. Having thus made his point, Yeats briefly left the play to the judgement of the audience without any sort of direct appeal. The performance proceeded and those who had come to hiss and hoot remained to applaud. Not only had the play been saved from attack by Yeats's beautifully balanced little speech but it had been helped to achieve popularity. With Yeats's interpretation in mind, audiences continued for years to receive it warmly every time it was revived and for a period it ranked almost equal, as a patriotic stimulant, with Yeats's own *Kathleen ni Houlihan* and Gregory's *The Rising of the Moon*.

That was the first time I felt the influence of Yeats's personality. I was full of admiration for the way he handled the situation, for his poise, for the phraseology in which he presented his argument and for the total effect of his brief statement, upon the audience.

I had, of course, frequently seen him in the front of the stalls. On my very first visit to the Abbey, when I was a couple of months over sixteen years of age, Yeats came to the rail which stood at the divide of the little stairs leading down to the stalls and leaned over it slowly scanning the audience as if he were looking for someone whom he expected to find in the auditorium. The man sitting next to me in the pit whispered that the poetic looking man who was running his eye over the audience was none other than Willie Yeats and that he was checking the box office returns by counting the number of people in each part of the house. So that even then, the story that the poet was a careful business man had become current.

I did not meet Yeats personally until he became a Senator. Because of a certain Gaelic League and Sinn Fein prejudice against him, because he did not esteem, or produce, straight practical political verse, I was inclined, in the beginning, to look upon him as something of a national backslider, a man who had been a thorough-going Nationalist, but who had excused himself from standing any longer in the front ranks in the struggle for Ireland's rights. But in 1913, I met Desmond Fitzgerald in Kerry. As an Irishman brought up in London, Desmond ascribed his national feelings and convictions to the influence of Yeats's poetry and I began to read it without my old Gaelic League prejudice. From the moment proposals for a Senate took definite shape, Desmond Fitzgerald was determined that Yeats should be invited to become a member. His proposal encountered no opposition in the Cabinet and Yeats was enrolled as a Senator.

He allied himself with what has generally been described as the ex-Unionist group, though it included James Douglas, Mrs. Alice Stopford Green, the historian, and Sam Brown, K.C., none of them Unionists. Its leader, however, if it could rightly be said to have had a leader, was Andrew Jameson. He had been head of the Irish Unionist Alliance and a redoubtable opponent of Home Rule, but he became a contented loyal citizen of the Free State on its establishment. It was natural that Yeats, back again for the first time for many years in active politics, should drift to this so-called ex-Unionist group. Most of its members were personally distinguished by reason of talent or influence and Yeats's romantic longing for aristocratic and authoritarian ways and standards made him feel at home in the circle which they formed. I should not say that his opinion carried great weight amongst them on general issues. But when he was on his ground he could, of course, bring the majority with him. For example, it was Yeats who secured the establishment of the Advisory Committee which recommended the designs for our coinage and it was he who guided its proceedings.

I do not think his contributions to the Senate debates on such questions as censorship and divorce influenced votes either in the House or amongst the electorate. In matters of the kind, decisions depended on deep currents of opinion and only a combination of the most influential members of the Dail able to command wide Party allegiance, could have modified the ultimate result. I presume, however, that Yeats spoke not with the idea of influencing decisions or shaping convictions, but simply to satisfy himself and in the hope of gratifying certain special groups.

Yeats showed an interest in the Blueshirt movement when it was at the pinnacle of its strength and wrote a marching song for it. But most of those associated with the movement disliked the song, with its refrain 'Hammer them Down' and Yeats, for his part, soon forgot about the organisation, which, in fact, had only a very brief period of vigour and began to feel itself superfluous when the Fianna Fail Government started to arrest members of the I.R.A. His move to help, or at least to encourage, the Blueshirts was, I think, Yeats's last political initiative. That he was an ardent unwavering patriot with the welfare and renown of Ireland constantly in his mind is beyond doubt. That he gave double service to his country is also clear. In the first place his high achievement as a writer glorified the land to which he was so obviously devoted. In the second place his treatment of Irish themes and his personal example of practical love of country inspired countless people with zeal for Irish nationality. He did more for Ireland working in his own way than he could have done by displaying the most consummate skill in organising voters, in drafting party programmes, and in conducting debates for the enlightenment of the electorate. His influence and the fruits of his labour spread very widely. That is exemplified in the theatre. While everyone knows of his responsibility for the founding and survival of the Abbey, not everyone knows that if the Abbey had not been established we should not have had the Gate Theatre either. And if we had not had the Gate, it is unlikely that we should have had the little theatres that are scattered over the city. Similarly in the higher national aspect of politics, Yeats has exercised and continues to exercise an indirect influence which extends far beyond the subjects and causes which he himself touched.

Earnán de Blaghd

Austin Clarke

The streets were bright with spring sunshine as I stole into the Abbey Theatre for the first time. I had hesitated so long at the corner, watching the last of the small crowd hurry to the Saturday matinee, that I was already several minutes late. In some vague way I had heard of Irish drama and its traditions, for knowledge of out-side affairs comes painfully and confusedly to a young student living in the shadow of examinations. Scarcely had the programme seller taken my ticket at the door of the pit when she disappeared into what seemed complete darkness. I groped my way after her, full of alarm and bewilderment, for from the Stygian gloom came the most lamentable outcry that I had ever heard in my life.

As I grasped the back of a seat and sank down, I could make out dimly on the stage two robed figures. When my eyes became accustomed to the gloom, I saw that they were standing before an immense locked gate. At first, in my confusion, I thought that this must be some ancient tragedy and that these two shadowy figures were stricken souls in Hades. But gradually I realised that they were shawled women and that this unabashed hullaballoo was the famous 'caoine'. It seemed to me as if the dismal muse of Irish history were present, adding her own groans to those embarrassing cries. The shock of that sudden encounter with Irish tradition was so great that to this day I cannot remember what play followed *The Gaol*

Gate by Lady Gregory. But the experience was so strange and exotic that I determined to return again.

In those years during the First Great War the literary tradition of the Abbey was not as yet in complete abeyance. The hilarity of farce was controlled, if not in kind, at any rate in time. The farces were shorter and were always preceded by a serious one-act play by Yeats: sometimes the order was reversed and farce was confined to the curtain-raiser. Inordinate laughter is so complete an experience in itself that we rarely remember what brought those stitches to our sides, those contradictory tears to our eyes. Memory requires some violent jolt from the past to stir it into activity. So I remember best of all that moment in *A Minute's Wait* when an infuriated goat held up the one-way traffic on the West Clare Railway. Did a welltrained billy-goat really rush across the stage, scattering market women, farmers and decrepit railway officials? Or was it only a scuffle in the wings which left that indelible moment of idiotic mirth in the mind?

But the plays of Yeats were a deeply imaginative experience, and, as the poet put on his own plays as often as possible, the experience was a constant one. On such occasions the theatre was almost empty. There were a few people in the stalls, including Lady Gregory, and, just after the last gong had sounded, Yeats would appear, dramatically, at the top of the steps leading down into the auditorium. Perhaps the actors spoke the lyric lines in tones that had become hollow-sounding with time, borrowing the archaic voice which is normally reserved for religious services. It seemed right that the poetic mysteries should be celebrated reverently and with decorum. Moreover, the presence of the poet himself in the theatre was a clear proof that all was well.

Scarcely had the desultory clapping ceased, when Yeats would appear outside the stage curtain, a dim figure against the footlights. He swayed and waved rhythmically, telling humbly of his 'little play', how he had re-written it, and what he had meant to convey in its lines. As the twenty or thirty people in the pit were more or less scattered, I was isolated usually in one of the back seats. On such occasions, I felt like Ludwig of Bavaria, that eccentric monarch, who sat alone in his own theatre. I enjoyed the poet's curtain-lecture, almost as if it were a special benefit performance for myself.

One night, however, my youthful and romantic illusions were suddenly shattered, and in a trice the Celtic Twilight was gone. As the poet appeares punctually outside the curtain, a dazzling light shone around him. It might have been the light of his later fame! I glanced up and saw that the brilliant shaft of illumination came from the balcony. A spotlight must have been clamped to the rail and switched on as the poet appeared. But my conclusion may have been unjust, for in youth we do not understand the complexities of human motives. I did not realise at the time that poetic drama was slowly vanishing from the Abbey Theatre. It seems to me now that, consciously or not, the poet might have been making a last despairing gesture to call attention, not to his own picturesque person, but to the struggling cause of poetry on the stage.

I saw a performance of *The Countess Kathleen* only once. The very first lines have a simplicity and imaginative quality that is new:

Mary: What can have made the grey hen flutter so?
Teigue: They say that now the land is famine-struck
   The graves are walking.
Mary: What can the hen have heard?
Teigue: And that is not the worst; at Tubber-vanach
   A woman met a man with ears spread out
   And they moved up and down like a bat's wings.
Mary: What can have kept your father all this while?
Teigue: Two nights ago, at Carrick-orus churchyard
   A herdsman met a man who had no mouth,
   Nor eyes, nor ears; his face a wall of flesh;
   He saw him plainly by the light of the moon.
Mary: Look out, and tell me if your father's coming.
The words spoken by Aleel and the Countess Kathleen are both lyrical and dramatic.
Kathleen: He bids me to go
   Where none of mortal creatures but the swan
   Dabbles, and there you would pluck the harp, when the trees
   Had made a heavy shadow about our door,
   And talk among the rustling of the reeds,
   When night hunted the foolish sun away
   With stillness and pale tapers. No – No – No!
   I cannot. Although I weep, I do not weep
   Because that life would be most happy, and here
   I find no way, no end. Nor do I weep
   Because I had longed to look upon your face,
   But that a night of prayer has made me weary.

I like best the sparse language of *The King's Threshold,* a play which, despite the critics, I have always thought dramatically effective on the stage.

Seanchan: Yes, yes, go to the hurley, go to the hurley,
    Go to the hurley! Gather up your skirts —
    Run quickly! You can remember many love songs:
    I know it by the light that's in your eyes —
    But you'll forget them. You're fair to look upon.
    Your feet delight in dancing, and your mouths
    In the slow smiling that awakens love.
    The mothers that have borne you mated rightly.
    They'd little ears as thirsty as your ears
    For many love songs. Go to the young men.
    Are not the ruddy flesh and the thin flanks
    And the broad shoulders worthy of desire?
    Go from me! Here is nothing for your eyes.
    But it is I that am singing you away —
    Singing you to the young men.

No doubt the poet schould have written hurling instead of hurley, which is the stick or comaun. I had not realised at the time that 'ruddy' and 'lineaments', which is used later in the play, were favourite words of Blake. And here are some well known lines from *On Baile's Strand:*-

    You have never seen her. Ah! Conchubar, had you seen her
    With that high, laughing, turbulent head of hers
    Thrown backward, and the bowstring at her ear,
    Or sitting at the fire with those grave eyes
    Full of good counsel as it were with wine,
    Or when love ran through all the lineaments

Of her wild body – although she had no child,
None other had all beauty, queen or lover,
Or was so fitted to give birth to kings.

The most exciting play which I saw in those early days at the Abbey Theatre was, ironically enough, not an Irish one, but a Continental experiment in dramatic impressionism. It was *Hannelle* by Gerhart Hauptmann, a play in two scenes. When it first appeared in the 'nineties' this small play caused a sensation. It infuriated critics in Paris as a sample of German infantilism, and was denounced as blasphemous in New York. It depicts, with all the relentless compassion of Hauptmann, the delirium of a child rescued from drowning and brought to a workhouse hospital. Reality and hallucination mingled in the strange scenes, sacred and profane figures dissolved into one another. It was all a confused blur to me at the time, but I realised instinctively that the play was a protest against the oppression of the young and that insidious sense of spiritual guilt which is instilled by custom into the adolescent mind. It was a first glimpse of analytical drama. Another memorable experience was the production of *The Post Office,* by Rabindranath Tagore. His play expressed religious intimations, not with that familiar emotionalism which dulls understanding, but in new images, cool, clear and surprising.

I was fortunate in catching the last of that imaginative movement which inspired so many writers here and, in seeing most of Yeats's plays before they disappeared from the theatre he had founded. So I remember gratefully that sunlit Saturday when I stole into the Abbey Theatre, for the first time and heard with astonishment the wailing women.

2

The centenary of Thomas Davis in 1914 was to be held at Trinity College, Dublin, but the meeting was banned by the Provost, Dr. Mahaffy and in scornful words, which caused much indignation to Republicans, he referred to 'a man called Pearse' who was to be one of the speakers. So the meeting was held in the Ancient Concert Rooms in Brunswick Street, later to be re-named Pearse Street after the Insurrection.

The long dusty hall downstairs was almost filled when I arrived but I found a seat half way down. Already on the platform were W.B. Yeats, who was to deliver the oration, Pádraic Pearse and the young chairman, Denis Gwynn. One chair was still empty. I scarcely recognised the poet of the Abbey Theatre whom I had seen so often coming before the dim footlights on the stage after one of his plays had been performed. Gone were the flowing tie and the disobedient black lock that fell over his brow as he talked and swung back into place whenever he lifted his head. He was in evening dress and his long hair had been oiled and brushed back. This gave a saturnine look to his olive features so that he seemed to be extraordinarily like Sir Edward Carson, who was then the fearsome Dublin-born leader of the Unionist party in the North. Scarcely had Yeats started to speak when, on the right-hand side of the hall, there was a sound of heavy footsteps on the bare boards. It was the missing poet, Captain Thomas Kettle, braving us in the uniform of a British Officer. He marched up the hall so firmly that we almost seemed to hear the clatter of his sword but it was obvious that he had his fill of Irish whiskey in order that he might defy more confidently this small group of Sinn Feiners.

When Yeats rose to speak, I wondered how he would deal with the poetic problem of the Young Ireland School of the 'Forties' the rhetoric of those political and historical ballads of Davis, D'Arcy Magee, Gavan Duffy and other poets whom he had attacked – the jingle of their double rhymes, of which perhaps the worst was the constant rhyming of 'Ireland' with 'Sireland'. But the poet had been wily enough to choose the one poem by Davis which could lend itself to his own thrilling sort of chanting: *The Lament for Owen Roe*. As he rose to his full height, swayed and, with waving hands, intoned the poem, his voice spread in rhythmic waves throughout the hushed hall. 'Did they dare, did they dare, to slay Eoghan Ruadh O'Neill? Yes, they slew with poison, him they feared to meet with steel.' 'May God wither up their hearts! May their blood cease to flow! May they walk in living death, who poisoned Eoghan Ruadh!' The audience was overcome with enthusiasm and when he sat down again there was great applause. But before that there had been as much clapping when, by a simple device which I noticed at the time, he brought in irrelevantly the name of Nietzsche, for the German poet and philosopher of the Superman was regarded with horror in all our pro-British press during the First Great

War. I felt annoyed for I had been reading with guilty deligt *Thus spoke Zarathustra, The Joyful Science* and *The Birth of Tragedy* with its fascinating theory of Dionysiac and Apollonian moods.

Pádraic Pearse followed. I had only heard vaguely of him and of St. Enda's, the school which he had at Rathfarnham, one of the few lay schools left in Ireland. This forlorn experiment had been resented by the Archbishop, who refused to appoint a chaplain for the pupils. There, with his sculptor brother, William, Thomas MacDonagh, Pádraic Colum and other poets, he taught and there was no corporal punishment as in the religious schools throughout the country. Even to-day, although it is illegal, cane or leather are used in National schools, colleges and convents.

Tall, pale, aloof, dressed in a black suit, Pearse spoke with an intense lofty devotion which stirred me uneasily for it was a cold impassioned rhetoric which was new to me, and carefully declaimed. Later he expanded the thesis of his brief speech in his essay on Davis which is one of the four pamphlets called *Tracts for the Times.* In this he wrote – and I am almost certain that he spoke the words at that meeting in the Ancient Concert Rooms in 1914:- 'The real Davis must have been a greater man even than the Davis of the essays, or the Davis of the songs. In literary expression Davis was immature; in mind he was ripe beyond all his contemporaries. I cannot call him a very great prose writer; I am not sure that I can call him a poet at all. But I can call him a very great man, one of our greatest men. None of his contemporaries had any doubt about his greatness. He was the greatest influence among them, and the noblest influence; and he has been the greatest and noblest influence in Irish history since Tone. He was not Young Ireland's most powerful prose writer; Mitchel was that. He was not Young Ireland's truest poet, Mangan was that, or, if not Mangan, Ferguson. He was not Young Ireland's ablest man of affairs: Duffy was that. He was not Young Ireland's most brilliant orator: Meagher was that. Nevertheless "Davis was our true leader" said Duffy: and when Davis died – the phrase is again Duffy's "it seemed as if the sun had gone out of the heavens" "The loss of this rare and noble Irishman" said Mitchel, "has never been repaired, neither to his country nor to his friends'" And Pearse added:– 'The Romans had a noble word which summed up all moral beauty and all private and civic valour: the word *virtus*. If English had as noble a word as that it would be the word to apply to the thing which made Thomas Davis so great a man.'

When Captain Kettle rose to speak a tumult broke out at the back of the hall and a tall red-bearded man, who looked like Darrell Figgis, jumped to his feet angrily shouting. Captain Kettle, who was to die so soon as the Battle of the Somme, kept shouting in reply to the hecklers: 'Where was your father when mine was in prison?' The miseries of the Land War, the ramming of clay cottages, the evictions, boycotting and shooting of landlords from behind hedges with buckshot, the assassinations in the Phoenix Park of the Secretary for Ireland and his companion, were around us. The vision was all the more vivid because my father had once brought me to see Skin-the-Goat, who had driven the assassins to the park. He had been given a job as night-watchman by the grateful alderman of the city.

When the meeting was over and I came out, I saw W.B. Yeats surrounded by disciples and watched the group walking towards Westland Row. The next morning the placards appeared with the startling announcement: *Dublin audience cheers Nietzsche.*

3

When I came to the little town of Gort, the ancient royal stories of Guaire and Maravan vanished from my mind as night fell. I can only remember the empty market place that seemed to lie in wait for a fair, three melancholy foreigners who had come there to sell native frieze, and a girl who stared into nothingness with a brazen face.

The morning sun was still clouded when I saw for the first time the Woods of Coole. I found a small unlocked gate and in a few minutes I stood within a dark plantation that was lit only be the cold sharp silver of the hollies. I wondered if it were the nameless 'wicked wood' of the poem or shady Kyle-dortha. Hastening along a winding, foot-beaten track, I came into a thinner wood, and as I waited there, I grew aware that there was secret honey around me. This surely must be Pairc-na-carraig.

Where the wild bees fling their sudden frangrances
    On the green air.
I had only known those deeper woods of the south, in

which the very dews stir heavily from a footstep: but in those thin western woods every tiny sound of the leaves was delicate. In great delight I moved softly there and not without scruples, for I was trespassing in the solitude where the poet had found so much of his inspiration. The trees had become darker, wilder again, and, because I could see a sunnier wood beyond them, I stayed under those boughs. If I remained here long enough the unexpected might happen, for I was certain that I had come to that secret place –

Dim Pairc-na-tarav, where enchanted eyes
Have seen immortal, wild, proud shadows walk.

I closed my eyes but nothing happened. Then, as I opened them again, I thought I saw a rich blue gleam dart through the distant leaves. I could not be mistaken and so I strode forward cautiously. A moment later I saw the blue flash again. Perhaps it was only a peacock searching in the grasses, but why was it moving so rapidly? Coming nearer, I peeped through the leaves and saw, to my chagrin, that I had mistaken for bird or spirit a tall sportsman, wearing an unusual rain-coat of sky-blue watered silk, and carrying the rods and fierce tackle of his craft. Believing that I had strayed into the wrong demesne and that I had been dreaming foolishly in ordinary woods, I was about to turn away, when I noticed that the angler was crossing a wide lawn towards the portico of a Georgian mansion. To my complete astonishment, I saw that it was the poet himself.

Bewildered by that unexpected encounter, I hurried through the underwoods and, in a few minutes, had lost my way. I came to long paths, grass-grown, hedged with wild pale privet. I wandered up and down in confusion for, though I was at the end of the woods, I no longer wanted to count them. At last I escaped from these hedges, where wildness was only neglect, and found myself on grey ledges of rock that dwindled among a few rushes growing by a small lake. Across the water was another wood. This must be Shan-walla, but I saw with a pang that the wild swans had gone.

I sat down on a rock near the water's edge, but mocking thoughts midged me from every side. The week before, I had crossed Lough Gill and, with great persistence and guile, had asked the boatman the name of every island we passed. As we came to the far end of the lake, he pointed to a rocky islet with high tufts of heather, a few sloe bushes and a small patch of grass, and he had said:

'That's Innisfree'.

I could hear his voice again and it had become horribly confidential.

'Would you believe it now, two ladies came here last year all the way from London to see that rock. They said it must be Innisfree, and that there was a poem written about it, though, round here, it is known as Rat Island. They brought their lunch with them, and stayed there for two solid hours, writing postcards to their friends.'

Crude coloured postcards with fragments of scrawled exclamations danced before my sight and, like those cards that Alice saw in Wonderland, they became suddenly shrill and in a pack they ran against me and the woods grew harsh with magpies and, stumbling blindly through brambles, I hurried along the grass-grown paths again. I came at length to some outbuildings. A man was standing with a bucket and brush outside a stable door. He told me that Mr. Yeats was staying in a house on the opposite side of the road and that in a week or two he was going to Ballylee. I had heard that the poet had acquired an Old Norman keep there.

The sun hid suddenly, and a fairy wind blew me, hat in hand, across the road. But the eddy of dust was gone even while I hesitated before the knocker.

Somehow I found myself in a plain room timidly picking at a fish and wondering if the poet had caught it himself. His own lunch was over and so he leaned from a sofa opposite the table, wearing a brown velvet shooting-jacket. A pallid mask of his features stared blindly from a glass case in the corner of the room.

'The imagination must be disciplined, when it is young. Therefore study the Jacobean lyrics, Donne, the poems of Landor...'

His voice rose and fell in a lulling monotone, while secretly I cursed the fish. It might have come from the cauldron of the elder gods, might have held the very smelt of knowledge, for, despite my desperate efforts, it would not grow smaller, and its tiny stickles seemed to threaten my very existence.

'Verse should be ascetic, the beauty of bare words...'

While he was speaking I seized the opportunity of pushing away the bewitched plate very gently.

'Master,' I said to myself in youthful enthusiasm, for I felt in happier mood, 'must not poetry sow its wild oats?'

I could hear that inner voice, despite me, imitating his chanting tone. But aloud I asked some polite question, to which he replied:

'Poetry needs the symbolic, that which has been moulded by many minds. The Japanese, when they hold their sacred processions, are accustomed to disguise themselves in the grotesque masks and armour of their ancestors...'

'I want,' he said later on, 'to see a neo-Catholic school of young poets in this country.' He spoke of Jammes, Peguy and Claudel, and said much that I could not follow at the time, for I had been cast into a mild trance by the gleam of the great signet upon his waving hand. I could not help watching that tremendous ring for I thought at the time that it had been fashioned by an artist of the Renaissance. But even in that trance I was trying to defend myself from the religious novelty which he was evolving. How could we learn to write the traditional songs of repentance before we had known those 'morry sins' of which Synge had spoken? I thought of the extravagant Gaelic poetry of the eighteenth century. Once more the strapping heroine of *The Midnight Court* was railing again aged bridegrooms, denouncing the celibacy of the clergy. She was proving to her own satisfaction that it was heretical for these tonsured young men to live in a state of single bliss. Once more the Mangaire Sugach was reeling from another parish with a satire on his tongue and, in a distant tavern, O Tuomy was filling his till with the fine words of his fellow craftsmen.

'I have to catch a train at four o'clock,' exclaimed the poet, hastily rising from the sofa.

The sun was shining again, here and there, among the seven woods when we came to the door. As I stood with downcast head upon the threshold he must have noticed my depression, despite his short sight. For suddenly he cried above me in majestic tones:

'You must come and see me again, when I am in my castle!'

Austin Clarke

THE THOMAS DAVIS LECTURES

Available in Paperback

If you would be interested to receive
announcements of forthcoming publications
send your name and address to

THE MERCIER PRESS
4 Bridge Street.
Cork, Ireland.